THE **7** CONTINENTS

NORTH AMERICA

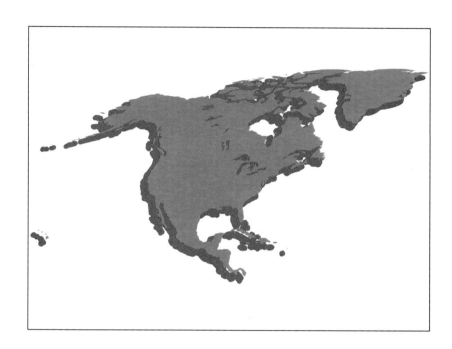

APRIL PULLEY SAYRE

TWENTY-FIRST CENTURY BOOKS
BROOKFIELD, CONNECTICUT

For Bland and Nelda Richardson, two extraordinary people with a deep appreciation of North America.

—A.P.S.

Published by Twenty-First Century Books
A Division of The Millbrook Press, Inc.
2 Old New Milford Road
Brookfield, Connecticut 06804

Library of Congress Cataloging-in-Publication Data
Sayre, April Pulley.
North America / April Pulley Sayre.
p. cm. — (The seven continents)
Includes bibliographical references and index.
Summary: Describes unique characteristics of the North American continent including
its landscapes, geology, weather, oceans, coastlines, air and
soil, plants, animals, and people.
ISBN 0-7613-3226-X (lib. bdg.)
1. North America—Juvenile literature. [1. North America.] I. Title.
II. Series: Sayre, April Pulley. Seven continents.
E38.5.S39 1998
917—dc21   97-27266
                                                   CIP
                                                   AC

Printed in the United States of America
1 3 5 4 2

Photo Credits

Cover photograph courtesy of Minden Pictures (© Carr Clifton)

Photographs courtesy of The National Audubon Society Collection/Photo Researchers: pp. 8 (© Kent & Donna Dannen), 22 (© Charlie Ott), 36 (© John J. Bangma); SuperStock: pp. 14 (© H. Kanus), 29 (© D. Forbert), 46 (© K. Kummels), 54; Woodfin Camp & Associates: pp. 17 (© Eastcott/Momatiuk), 32 (© Craig Aurness), 39 (© Robert Frerck), 51 (© Gary Braasch), 53 (© Catherine Karnow); Animals Animals/Earth Scenes: pp. 19 (© David C. Fritts), 27 (© Zig Leszczynski), 42 (right © Patti Murray), 48 (© M. Fogden); Visuals Unlimited: pp. 21 (© Charles McCrae), 42 (left © R.W. Gerling); Liaison International: pp. 24 (© Wernher Krutein), 31 (© Bill Gillette); Minden Pictures: p. 41 (© Mark Moffett).

CONTENTS

INTRODUCTION

CONTINENTS: WHERE WE STAND

The ground you stand on may seem solid and stable, but it's really moving all the time. How is that possible? Because all of the earth's continents, islands, oceans, and people ride on tectonic plates. These plates, which are huge slabs of the earth's crust, float on top of hot, melted rock below. One plate may carry a whole continent and a piece of an ocean. Another may carry only a few islands and some ocean. The plates shift, slide, and even bump together slowly as the molten rock below them flows.

Plate edges are where the action is, geologically speaking. That's where volcanoes erupt and earthquakes shake the land. Tectonic plates collide, gradually crumpling continents into folds that become mountains. Dry land, or ocean floor, can be made at these plate edges. Melted rock, spurting out of volcanoes or oozing out of cracks between plates, cools and solidifies. Dry land, or ocean floor, can also be destroyed here, as the edge of one tectonic plate slips underneath another. The moving, grinding plates create tremendous pressure and heat, which melts the rock, turning it into semisolid material.

Continents, the world's largest landmasses, the rock rafts where we live, ride on this shifting puzzle of tectonic plates. These continents are made of material that floated to the surface when much of the earth was hot and liquid long ago. The floating material then cooled and became solid. Two hundred fifty million years ago there was only one continent, the supercontinent Pangaea, surrounded by one ocean, Panthalassa. But since then, the tectonic plates have moved, breaking apart the continents and rearranging them. Today there are seven continents: North America, South America, Europe, Asia, Africa, Australia, and Antarctica.

5

250 Million Years Ago

Two hundred and fifty million years ago there were only one continent and one ocean, as shown above. (Rough shapes the continents would eventually take are outlined in black.) The view below shows where the seven continents are today. These positions will continue to change slowly as tectonic plates shift.

Present Day

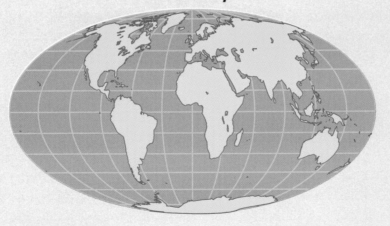

Each continent has its own unique character and conditions, shaped by its history and position on the earth. Europe, which is connected to Asia, has lots of coastline and moist ocean air. Australia, meanwhile, is influenced by its neighbor, Antarctica, which sends cool currents northward to its shores. North America and South America were once separated, but are now connected by Panama. Over the years, animals, from ancient camels to armadillos, have traveled the bridge in between these two continents.

A continent's landscape, geology, weather, and natural communities affect almost every human action taken on that continent, from planting a seed to waging a war. Rivers become the borders of countries. Soil determines what we can grow. Weather and climate affect our cultures—what we feel, how we dress, even how we celebrate.

Understanding continents can give us a deeper knowledge of the earth—its plants, animals, and people. It can help us see behind news headlines to appreciate the forces that shape world events. Such knowledge can be helpful, especially in a world that's constantly changing and shifting, down to the very earth beneath our feet.

Maroon Lake reflects snow-covered mountains and low hills in the Snowmass Wilderness, White River National Forest, above Aspen, Colorado.

ONE

NORTH AMERICA: EXTREMES AND IN-BETWEENS

If you're looking for extremes, you can find them in North America. On Greenland's glaciers you could freeze in air temperatures as low as −105°F (−76°C). Or you could bake in the egg-frying heat of Death Valley, California, whose record high is 134°F (57°C)! For other highs and lows, you might climb Alaska's Mount McKinley, the continent's highest mountain—almost 4 miles (more than 6 kilometers) to the top. Then you could check out Nova Scotia's Bay of Fundy, home of the world's highest tide, which surges into the bay at 49 feet (15 meters) above low tide!

High-low, hot-cold, rainy, snowy, dry: North America has its share of extremes. Fortunately for North Americans, it also has conditions in between. With just the right amount of sun and rain, coffee grows in Costa Rica, oranges in Florida, grapes in California, corn in Iowa, and wheat in Saskatchewan. Meanwhile, the Atlantic Ocean near the Bahamas is just the right temperature for coral reefs to thrive. North America's wide range of environmental conditions makes possible a spectacular variety of life. Jaguars roam rain forests. Eagles soar over grasslands. Polar bears hunt seals on Arctic ice. Alligators swim in southern swamps. And possums curl up in leafy trees.

WHAT IS NORTH AMERICA?

North America is the third-largest continent on earth, after Asia and Africa. It consists of Canada, Greenland, the United States (including Alaska but excluding Hawaii), Mexico, the West Indies, and Central America (between Mexico and South America).

As you can see on a map, Greenland, many Canadian islands, and islands of the West Indies are separated from the North American mainland by ocean water. Yet these islands are still considered part of the continent, because they sit on the continental shelf, an underwater extension of the continent covered by shallow seas. In contrast, the state of Hawaii, 2,400 miles (3,850 kilometers) southwest of California, is a group of oceanic islands. It is not a part of North America or any other continent.

North America covers a broad area. It extends over 4,600 miles (7,400 kilometers) from the chilly Arctic to the steamy Tropics, and it wraps east-west around almost a third of the Northern Hemisphere. In the north, the continent is so wide you'd have to walk 4,900 miles (7,840 kilometers) to get from Alaska to Newfoundland. At its southern tip, the continent narrows dramatically. From the Caribbean Sea across the Isthmus of Panama to the Pacific Ocean is only 30 miles (48 kilometers)!

MAKING SENSE OF NORTH AMERICA

With mountains, canyons, hot springs, glaciers, waterfalls, and other wonders, North America's topography—its surface features—can be mind-boggling at first. It helps to think of North America as having three major sections: the western mountains, the eastern mountains, and the flatlands in between. Western North America, from Alaska to Panama, is wrinkled and folded with high mountain ranges such as the Rocky Mountains. Stretching across the middle of the continent is the Great Plains, a broad, relatively flat area that runs from northern Canada to southern Texas. Eastern North America is dominated by the Appalachians, a much lower, worn-down mountain range.

Once you have these areas in mind, you can fill in details. The Great Plains includes North America's prairies, its most fertile farmland, and is drained by the Mississippi-Missouri River system. Although generally flat, the plains also contain gently rolling hills. Additional flat areas lie to the east, where lowlands such as swamps, marshes, and sandy areas skirt the coast from New England, south to Florida, west to Texas, and south again to Mexico's Yucatán Peninsula. Up north is another relatively flat area, the Canadian Shield, a tremendous crescent-shaped area of ancient rock that slopes slightly toward Hudson Bay.

The mountainous west looks as if a giant folded the land into wrinkles and ridges. These enormous folds are mountain ranges: the Rockies, the Cascades, the Coast Mountains, the Sierra Madres, and the Sierra Nevadas. Mexico and Central America are particularly mountainous, with many active volcanoes. All these western mountains are considered part of the Cordillera, a backbone of mountains that runs from Alaska through Central America, all the way to the southern tip of South America. The Cordillera is the widest and longest chain of mountains on earth.

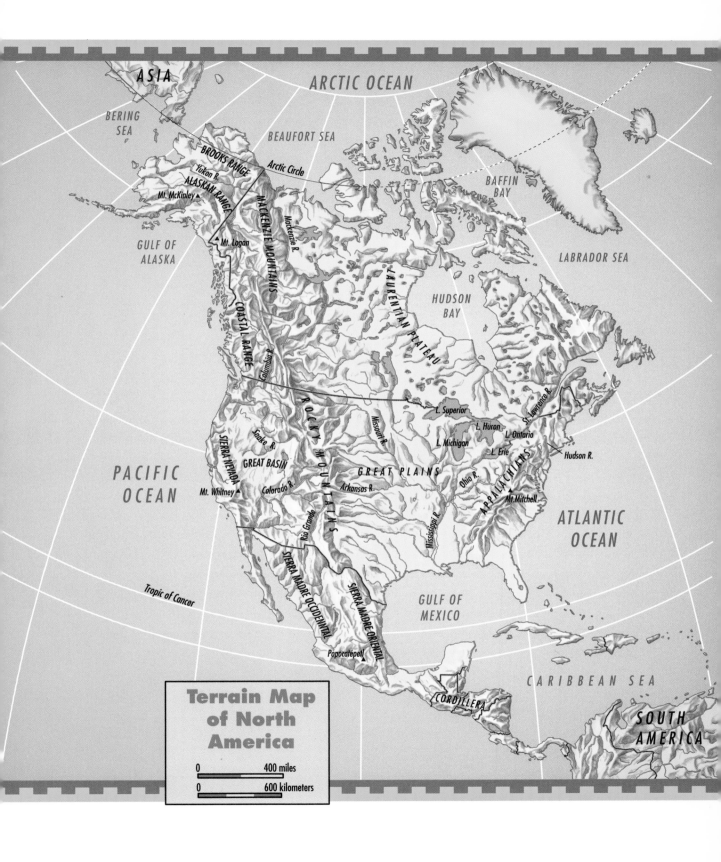

ASIA

ARCTIC OCEAN

BERING
SEA

BEAUFORT SEA

BROOKS RANGE

Arctic Circle

Yukon R.

ALASKAN RANGE

Mt. McKinley ▲

MACKENZIE MOUNTAINS

Mackenzie R.

▲ Mt. Logan

GULF OF
ALASKA

BAFFIN
BAY

LABRADOR SEA

COASTAL RANGE

Columbia R.

LAURENTIAN PLATEAU

HUDSON
BAY

ROCKY MOUNTAINS

Snake R.

SIERRA NEVADA

GREAT BASIN

Missouri R.

L. Superior

L. Huron

L. Ontario

St. Lawrence R.

L. Michigan

L. Erie

Hudson R.

PACIFIC
OCEAN

GREAT PLAINS

Mt. Whitney ▲

Colorado R.

Arkansas R.

Ohio R.

APPALACHIANS

Mt. Mitchell ▲

ATLANTIC
OCEAN

Mississippi R.

Río Grande

Tropic of Cancer

SIERRA MADRE OCCIDENTAL

SIERRA MADRE ORIENTAL

GULF OF
MEXICO

Popocatépetl ▲

CARIBBEAN SEA

CORDILLERA

SOUTH
AMERICA

Terrain Map of North America

| 0 | 400 miles |
| 0 | 600 kilometers |

North America is an angler's dream. It has plenty of water resources—coastlines, rivers, and lakes. For starters, the continent lies in between three oceans: the Pacific Ocean to the west, the Atlantic Ocean to the east, and the Arctic Ocean to the north. To the south, its wavy coastline hugs the Gulf of Mexico and borders the Caribbean Sea. To the north, Alaska and Canada border the Beaufort Sea. Another important ocean access is Canada's Hudson Bay.

Inland, North America has an abundance of lakes. Perhaps the best known are the five Great Lakes: Superior, Michigan, Huron, Erie, and Ontario. Except for Lake Michigan, which is entirely in the United States, these lakes are shared by the United States and Canada. Canada also has Great Bear Lake, Great Slave Lake, and Lake Winnipeg, plus many smaller lakes. There are more than four hundred thousand lakes in the province of Quebec alone. Canada has so many lakes that no one has ever counted them all, but by geographers' estimates, it has the most lakes of any country on earth. Other large, famous North American lakes include the Great Salt Lake of Utah and Lake Nicaragua, in the Central American country of Nicaragua.

North America has three major river systems. The longest, the Mississippi-Missouri, flows 3,860 miles (6,211 kilometers), carrying water from the central United States all the way to the Gulf of Mexico below New Orleans, Louisiana. A second major system, the Mackenzie and Slave Rivers, flows northwest through Canada into the Beaufort Sea. The third river system contains the Great Lakes, which are all connected. Water from small rivers flows into the Great Lakes and out through the St. Lawrence River and Seaway into the Atlantic Ocean. Together the five Great Lakes cover 95,000 square miles (247,000 square kilometers) and contain one-fifth of the world's freshwater!

Important Influences on the Continent of North America

• The northern areas of the continent—Alaska, Canada and Greenland—have been strongly affected by glaciers, giant rivers of slow-moving ice. Thousands of years ago, glaciers covered most of these areas, and still cover some of them today. Greenland's interior is completely covered by ice.

• Pressure from the Pacific Plate and other tectonic plates (large pieces of the earth's crust) has pushed the continent into folds—the mountains of the West and of Central America. The movement of these plates causes earthquakes and the formation of volcanoes.

• Central America has a rocky backbone of over a hundred volcanoes. It is the most geologically active region in North America, with frequent earthquakes and volcanic eruptions.

• North America has a wide range of biomes (habitats), including tropical rain forest, tropical deciduous forest, desert, prairie, temperate rain forest, temperate deciduous forest, taiga, tundra, and polar desert.

WORLD RECORDS HELD BY NORTH AMERICA

- Largest freshwater lake: Lake Superior, surface area 31,700 square miles (82,103 square kilometers)
- Largest island: Greenland, 840,000 square miles (2,175,600 square kilometers)
- Largest tidal difference: Bay of Fundy, Canada: 49 feet (15 meters) from low to high tide
- Oldest living organisms: Great Basin Bristlecone Pines in Nevada, Utah, and California: life span of 4,600 years

STATISTICS AND RECORDS FOR THE CONTINENT OF NORTH AMERICA

- Area: 9,348,000 square miles (24,211,000 square kilometers), about one-sixth of the world's land
- Population: 458 million
- Largest lake: Lake Superior, surface area 31,700 square miles (82,103 square kilometers)
- Longest river system: Mississippi-Missouri River, 3,860 miles (6,211 kilometers) long
- Lowest point: Death Valley, California, 282 feet (86 meters) below sea level
- Highest point and highest mountain: Mt. McKinley, Alaska: 20,320 feet (6,195 meters)
- Highest waterfall: Yosemite Falls, 2,425 feet (739 meters)

The edge of the Jakobshaven Glacier stands like an enormous monument along the Greenland coast.

TWO

NORTHERN LANDS: GREENLAND, ALASKA, AND CANADA

If you fly over Alaska, northern Canada, and Greenland, you'll see a landscape unlike those farther south. You'll see lots of ice and water. You'll see mountains and plains. You'll see snakelike ridges of gravel and glacier-carved fjords. Frozen oceans, snowy tundra, and vast green forests extend for miles. The lakes and mountains of this region are some of the least explored and least polluted on earth. Much of the land is wilderness, left to the polar bears, caribou, and wolves, but scattered cities, towns, roads, and houses dot the region, especially to the south.

THE LAY OF THE LAND

Greenland, the world's largest island, is one of the coldest places on earth. Despite its name, most of Greenland is not green. Eighty-five percent of the island is covered by glaciers—layers of ice that are 1–2 miles (1.6–3.2 kilometers) thick. These glaciers are the remnants of a much larger ice sheet that covered North America forty thousand years ago.

Glaciers form when snow falls and does not melt, year after year. The snow builds up, its weight pressing down on earlier layers, which turn into a dense type of ice called firn. Gravity and the weight of the ice make glaciers flow slowly downhill.

Glacier-covered Greenland got its name from an early attempt at false advertising. In A.D. 982, Eric the Red, a Norse explorer, wanted to lure immigrants to the island. So he gave Greenland its appealing, but misleading, name. Immigrants did come, most of them settling on the southwest coast, where plants can grow on a fringe of ice-free tundra. This settlement lasted several hundred years before dying out. In the 1700s, explorers from Denmark, guided by native people from the Arctic, surveyed and resettled the island. Because it lacks good cropland, fishing, raising sheep, and mining provide the main sources of income for residents. Denmark had long controlled Greenland, but in 1979 the Danes granted it home rule—the right to handle island-based affairs. Its Greenlandic name came into official use: Kalaallit Nunaat.

GLACIERS: GOING WITH THE FLOW

In addition to Greenland's glaciers, there are several hundred thousand glaciers in Alaska and Canada. Alaska has 31,000 square miles (more than 80,000 square kilometers) of glacier ice, enough to cover South Carolina. Some are continental glaciers which, like Greenland's glaciers, are the remainders of massive ice sheets that once covered North America. Other glaciers, called alpine glaciers, formed independently, high up on mountains where a lot of snow falls. Even where there are no glaciers today, much of the land has been marked by glaciers in the past.

How does a glacier shape the land? Think of a glacier as a very wide, slow-moving river of ice. In between mountains, a glacier may narrow like a river, or on flat land, it can spread out like spilled milk. Glaciers that spread out over large areas are also called ice sheets. As a glacier flows, rocks in its path get mixed in with the ice and are carried along. A glacier drops some of these rocks along the way, especially when it melts and recedes. Wherever it moves, a glacier scrapes soil off the land and leaves scratches on rock below. In North America, glaciers gouged out the tremendous shallow basins that became the Great Lakes.

Glaciers create many landforms. A glacier can carve a mountain valley. Fjords are glacier-carved valleys that have filled with seawater, forming inlets surrounded by steep cliffs. On Canada's Baffin and Ellesmere Islands, fjords provide cliffs where seabirds such as puffins nest. Another legacy of glaciers is prairie potholes, small lakes and wetlands scattered especially throughout the Canadian provinces of Manitoba, Alberta, and Saskatchewan; the Dakotas; and Minnesota. These wet areas are nesting and feeding sites for ducks and geese. Glaciers also form eskers, long gravel ridges that can be about 300 feet (90 meters) high and hundreds of miles (or kilometers) long. Bears and foxes often make their dens in eskers, which are less soggy and less easily flooded than surrounding low-lying tundra.

COLD TIMES AND WARM TIMES

A glacier grows bigger and spreads farther as long as enough snow falls to build up ice. This happens whenever yearly temperatures are cold. During the last ice age, when the

*The adage "Birds of a feather flock together" is certainly true of
these puffins, who appear to be watching an aerial show
along a northern cliff.*

earth was slightly colder, glaciers grew larger. Since the last ice age ended 8,000–10,000 years ago, the earth has warmed and glaciers have slowly retreated.

In recent years, glaciers have begun melting and retreating more and more rapidly. This is caused by global warming, an overall increase in the earth's temperature. Many scientists now believe global warming is due in part to the buildup of "greenhouse gases"—carbon dioxide, water vapor, methane, and chlorofluorocarbons—in the earth's atmosphere. Like the walls of a greenhouse, the earth's layer of these gases lets sunlight in, but doesn't let the sun's heat escape. (A similar process occurs inside a closed car on a sunny day, even in winter. The car's windows let sunlight in, but prevent much of the heat from escaping. The interior of the car heats up.) Carbon dioxide, one greenhouse gas, is released by cars, trucks, power lawn mowers, coal power plants, factories, forest fires, and many other sources.

The Deep Freeze

What do houses on stilts, gravel roads, and shallow-rooted plants have in common? They are all adaptations to permafrost—frozen ground—which is a fact of life in the Arctic. Permafrost, made of ice, rock, and soil, can be 2,000 feet (600 meters) deep. Only the top layer of soil thaws in summer. This top layer, called the active layer, is where the shallow roots of plants thrive, using the liquid water and nutrients in the soil. Deeper roots would not do any good because they could not use the frozen water.

Permafrost keeps rain and melted snow from seeping down out of reach of plant roots. But permafrost can also cause problems. Heat from houses resting directly on permafrost warms the soil, melting it until it slides down, causing the house to sink or buckle. To prevent this, people in Alaska and northern Canada build their houses on stilts or on a thick layer of gravel. The pieces of gravel and the air spaces between them keep the warm houses from touching the soil and melting the permafrost.

Facts of Life in the North

In the north, towns, cities, and people are few and far between. One reason is that living conditions are difficult. In Alaska, northern Canada, and Greenland, the weather is cold for many months. The growing season is short, and the soil is poor. In winter, the sun barely peeks over the horizon; so it can be dark almost all day.

Fortunately, in summer, the weather is warmer and hours of sunlight are plentiful. From late May to early August, the sun hardly sets near Barrow, Alaska. The sky is light even at midnight. It gets quite warm, up in the 60s (above 16°C), and 70s (above 21°C), so you could play baseball, bird-watch, and hike outdoors, almost all day!

The Canadian Shield

The Canadian Shield is not the kind of shield a knight would carry into battle. (It's way too heavy, for one thing!) The Canadian Shield, also called the Precambrian Shield, is an immense, horseshoe-shaped region of rock that curves around Hudson Bay. The shield extends from the Mackenzie Basin in the west all the way east to Labrador and south to Minnesota and Wisconsin. This tremendous mass of solid bedrock is two to four billion years old and rich in minerals such as nickel, zinc, copper, platinum, cobalt, uranium, silver, and gold. Much of this mineral ore is mined. In places, the bedrock is covered by layers of rock or thin soil. Much of the area is wilderness, containing blue lakes, rushing streams, taiga, tundra, and squishy wetlands such as bogs and muskegs.

COLD NIGHTS, WILD LIGHTS

During some long winter nights, there's a light show in northern skies. The sky is streaked with red, white, blue, and green, as if an artist had painted it. These colors, called the aurora borealis, or northern lights, can last for several minutes. Strangely enough, this nighttime show is actually caused by the sun. Electrically charged particles emitted by the sun are attracted to the earth's magnetic poles, the North Pole and South Pole. These particles collide with particles in the earth's atmosphere, creating the fluorescent colors people see. For the same reason, a similar show, called the aurora australis, or southern lights, is seen near the South Pole.

The aurora borealis— the northern lights— create a dramatic night sky over the wilderness of the far north.

SQUARE WHEELS AND PLUG-IN PARKING

Generally, the farther north you go in North America, the colder the temperatures. A winter temperature of –2°F (–19°C) is average in Whitehorse, a town in northern Canada's Yukon Territory. Temperatures lower than –60 °F (–51°C) have been recorded there. In winter, it's so cold in Anchorage, Alaska, that cars have engine heaters to keep their engines warm at night or to warm them up in the morning. At some public parking spots, you can plug in the engine heater so the car won't freeze while you are doing your errands! A car sitting in a driveway overnight may end up with a flattened spot on the bottom of each tire, where the car's weight rested. The rubber freezes in this flattened shape. Driving on these squared-off wheels can be a bumpy experience!

YOUNG SOIL

Aside from the cold weather, there's another reason farming isn't widespread in the far north. Soil in much of the north is relatively shallow, young, and poor for farming. As gardeners know, good soil contains water, air spaces, tiny pieces of rock, decayed plants and animals, and living creatures such as worms, beetles, and tiny organisms. Plant roots, worms, fungi, and other organisms help develop good soil over decades, centuries, even millennia. Tundra and taiga soils, deposited by glaciers, have not had the time for the biological activity needed to fully develop into rich soil.

A WALK THROUGH NORTHERN BIOMES

Alaska, Canada, and Greenland have six major land biomes—areas with distinct climates and communities of animals and plants. These biomes are: polar desert, tundra, taiga, prairie, temperate deciduous forest, and temperate rain forest.

POLAR DESERT AND TUNDRA

At the iciest, most northern portion of North America you'll find polar desert, a dry, windy, bitter-cold biome with small clumps of low-growing plants. Just south of the polar desert is arctic tundra, where wolves hunt, and in summer, mosquitoes whine, caribou wander, musk-oxen graze, and snow geese tend their nests. Low-growing plants such as arctic poppies carpet the tundra with color. Walking is slow going because the ground is spongy, lumpy, and wet. In fall, the leaves of tundra plants turn beautiful shades of red and gold. Throughout the long winter, the land is icy, windy, and snow-covered. Not much snow falls, but what does fall rarely melts.

Flowering plants make the most of the short Arctic summer, carpeting the tundra with a striking array of color.

THE CONE ZONE: TAIGA

The arctic tundra biome ends where ragged stands of short, stunted trees begin. This is the treeline, the beginning of the transition to the taiga. Also called the boreal forest, or the northern coniferous forest, the taiga is a wide belt of forest that covers much of Alaska and Canada—and, across the ocean, Russia and Scandinavia. Lakes, ponds, streams, and wetlands such as bogs break up the dark-green forest. The forest itself is made up mostly of conifers, trees that bear cones, such as pines. Most conifers, such as spruce, fir, and pine, are also evergreen. Their narrow, needlelike leaves stay green throughout the year, and only a few drop at a time. Taiga also contains birch, poplar, and aspen trees, which are broad-leaved and deciduous, meaning they lose their leaves, almost all at once, in fall. Animals that inhabit these forests include moose, black bears, brown bears, caribou, foxes, squirrels, porcupines, wolverines, ravens, chickadees, and minks.

AMONG GIANTS: THE TEMPERATE RAIN FOREST

In British Columbia, southeast Alaska, Washington State, and Oregon, lies a mossy, ancient forest that would be a perfect setting for fairy tales. Spotted owls hoot from trees high above. Clear, rushing salmon streams cascade over rocks. Bright-yellow banana slugs make glistening trails along the moist ground. The giants in these forests are trees. Some Douglas firs tower 150–295 feet (45–90 meters), as tall as a 25-story building.

In the taiga, small trees with needlelike leaves stretch almost as far as the eye can see—until they reach the mountains.

These trees have grown so big over two or three centuries, or maybe more. Very old red cedars, western hemlocks, Douglas firs, and sitka spruces grow large here, as well.

This forest of giants is the temperate rain forest. It's colder than the famous tropical rain forests of Central and South America, but like the tropical rain forests, this forest is extremely wet, and it is being rapidly destroyed. About 3 square miles (8 square kilometers) of forest are cut each day in British Columbia. The tall, wide trees are valuable for timber, which sells for a high price.

WHAT IS A TREE WORTH?

The highest-priced trees on the market are old trees, called old growth. They are valuable to the forest, too, even if they are dead or dying, because they help keep the rest of the forest alive.

When trees die, some remain upright. These standing dead trees, called snags, can become nesting sites for 53 different species of mammals and birds, including owls, woodpeckers, voles, squirrels, and wrens. Once a tree falls, it may become a "nurse" tree that helps new trees grow. Lichens and mosses rapidly develop on top of the fallen tree, breaking down its nutrients. Sometimes a new tree sprouts from a seed on top of the old tree, and gets nutrients from the nurse tree's rotting trunk.

Branches of fallen trees are useful, too. They shelter salamanders, frogs, and other small animals. When branches or entire trees fall into streams, the wood and leaves decompose and become covered with slimy green algae. Aquatic insects eat this algae. These aquatic insects, in turn, are eaten by trout. Dead and dying trees, it turns out, are very valuable, indeed!

HINTS OF TWO OTHER BIOMES

The northern edges of two other biomes—prairie and temperate deciduous forest—stretch into Canada, although they exist mostly in the lower forty-eight United States. In Ontario and Quebec, near the Great Lakes and St. Lawrence River and Seaway, are patches of temperate deciduous forest of maple, ash, and yellow birch. This is the same kind of forest that stretches across the eastern United States.

Canada also shares with the United States the great prairies of the Central Plains. The prairie, which is what North American grasslands are called, is discussed further in the next chapter. Prairie is found in parts of southern Alberta, Saskatchewan, and Manitoba—the "prairie provinces." Because of its deep, rich soil, much of the prairie has been converted to farmland for growing wheat and other crops. That's why the prairie region is nicknamed Canada's breadbasket.

WILD NORTHERN SIGHTS

Northern North America is a terrific place to see animals in the wild. You can take a boat off Grand Manan Island, Canada, to see humpback whales. You can rumble along in a tundra buggy—a tall, big-wheeled vehicle—in Churchill, Manitoba, for a safe look at polar bears. You can stand by a stream in coastal Alaska, watching salmon jump their way up a waterfall. Or you can soar in a plane, observing the journey of a 130,000-member caribou herd as it travels from Canada's taiga to the tundra on Alaska's coast.

Famed for their scenic wilderness and wildlife, Alaska, Canada, Greenland, and nearby islands are increasingly being changed by human industry and development. Air pollution hangs over some northern cities. Oil-drilling rigs and pipes poke up out of the arctic tundra. Beaches and waters are polluted by oil spills, such as the 11 million gallons (42 million liters) spilled in Prince William Sound, Alaska, by the tanker *Exxon Valdez* in 1989. In Quebec, the James Bay Project, one of the largest hydroelectric projects in the world, has flooded thousands of square miles (square kilometers) of taiga. Despite these troubles, a tremendous amount of wilderness remains unpolluted. Balancing a desire to preserve wild places with a desire for oil, minerals, and products of industry is a major challenge already facing residents of northern North America.

*In the aftermath of the San Francisco Bay earthquake of October 1989,
the building in the foreground stands in ruins while the one
in the background is untouched.*

THREE

FROM SEA TO SHINING SEA: THE LOWER FORTY-EIGHT UNITED STATES

In the movie *Great American Vacation*, starring Chevy Chase, a family tries to see America's natural wonders in a single trip. In real life, it would be impossible unless the trip lasted years. But it would be fun to try! Just imagine the possibilities. You could snorkel over a coral reef off Florida, then go alligator watching in a Louisiana swamp. You could hike the Appalachian trail to see spectacular spring wildflowers or fiery-colored fall trees. You could peek over the Grand Canyon's rim, then raft the Colorado River through its twisted canyons. You could cross-country ski past bison in Yellowstone National Park, then check out the starfish on the beaches of Washington State. A "great" American vacation could be anything from riding donkeys in the Arizona desert to picking blueberries on the coast of Maine. And that's only considering the wonders from one part of North America: the lower forty-eight United States.

FEATURES OF THE WEST

Natural wonders—flowing rivers, falling snow, crashing waves, swirling winds, and moving earth—can all become natural disasters when they hit hard close to home.

On October 17, 1989, at 5:04 P.M., baseball fans watching a World Series game at Candlestick Park in San Francisco, California, felt their seats shake. A strong earthquake, registering 7.1 on the Richter scale, had struck the area. The quake was felt from Los Angeles in the south to Oregon in the north, and east to Nevada. No one was injured at the stadium, but elsewhere in the Bay Area, sixty-three people were killed; almost four thousand people were injured; twenty-four thousand houses and apartments were damaged. Signs fell, houses crumbled, and the concrete upper deck of a freeway collapsed, crushing cars below.

ROCK THAT ROLLS

Earthquakes are common on the western side of North America, from Alaska to Panama. The west coast is earthquake-prone because it lies on the boundary between two tectonic plates. Where two tectonic plates meet, one of several things may happen. In a process called collision, the plates may press together; this can force the land they carry to crumple, forming mountains such as the Himalayas.

A second possibility is that one plate may slide over another, in a process called subduction. This is happening near Seattle, where the North American plate meets the Juan de Fuca plate. The Juan de Fuca, a dense, oceanic plate, is diving downward, underneath the continental crust of the less dense North American plate. The plate underneath is melted by heat and pressure from the plate above, forming molten rock. This molten rock builds up and then squirts out under pressure from volcanoes, such as Mount St. Helens in the Cascades, which erupted dramatically in 1980.

Tectonic plates may also slide past one another, in a process called faulting. Sliding along faults isn't smooth. Pieces of the plates often catch on one other. Pressure builds up until the plates suddenly thrust past each another, causing an earthquake. During these sudden movements, deep cracks called faults may form in the earth. The 750-mile (1,210-kilometer) San Andreas Fault, which runs from Southern California to San Francisco and beyond, is a fault boundary. Along this fault, the Pacific Plate is pushing the Los Angeles area and the Mexican peninsula of Baja California slowly to the northwest, at a rate of 2.4 inches (6 centimeters) per year. At this rate, in about ten million years, Los Angeles could be on an offshore island, about as far north as San Francisco, nearly 400 miles (600 km) away!

SHADOW OF THE RAIN

Seattle, Washington, and Portland, Oregon, are famous for their rain and fog. The rainy weather helps produce the tall, lush temperate rain forests of Washington's Olympic National Park. Yet just to the east, on the other side of the Cascades Mountains, the land is dry. How can one side of a mountain range be so wet, while the other side is so dry? Because of a "rain shadow" effect. An area is said to be in a rain shadow when a tall mountain range blocks its rain supply.

A rain shadow begins when warm air, which has picked up moisture from the ocean, blows onto the coast. When it hits mountains, it is forced to rise. As it rises, the air cools. (Air is usually cooler at high altitudes, which is why mountaintops are so cold.) Because cool air cannot hold as much water vapor as warm air, it must drop some of its water vapor along the way. This produces rain on the western side of the Cascades.

The Hoh Rain Forest is a temperate rain forest in Olympic National Park near the coast of Washington.

After the air mass has crossed the mountains to the eastern side, it has lost most of its load of moisture. The eastern side is even drier because the air begins to heat up as it comes down the mountain peaks. This warm, dry air can now hold much more water, so it acts like a sponge, soaking up any moisture from the land. Rain shadows occur all along the western United States. The rain shadow makes California's coast ranges wet and its central valley dry. The air then pushes eastward, up and over the Sierra Nevada range, losing more moisture, until it dries the Great Basin Desert, to the east.

AMERICA'S DESERTS

The western United States contains four deserts: the Great Basin, the Mojave, the Sonoran, and the Chihuahuan. Although these deserts receive less than 10 inches (25 centimeters) of precipitation per year and contain sand dunes, rocky areas, and strange landforms, overall they support more plants and animals than deserts elsewhere on earth. A scientist from Africa who visited the Sonoran Desert said it looked more like a garden than a desert. North America's deserts are home to treelike saguaro cacti, colorful wildflowers, and such animals as woodpeckers, kit foxes, kangaroo rats, spadefoot toads, and rattlesnakes.

The Great Basin and the Mojave are formed primarily by the rain shadow effect. The Sonoran and Chihuahuan Deserts, although affected by rain shadow, are also dry because of their position on earth. They are located in one of the subtropical belts, which occur around 30° latitude north and 30° latitude south of the equator. Because of the sun's uneven heating of earth, large, dry air masses descend and warm at these latitudes. As this air warms, it picks up moisture from the land, drying the air out and creating deserts.

ROCKY MOUNTAIN HIGH

If you climb a tall peak in the Rocky Mountains, you'll pass through several biomes, with different mixtures of animal and plant species. At the base of a mountain, you might be in a desert or a short grassland where there are cacti, small shrubs, coyotes, badgers, black-tailed jackrabbits, and sagebrush lizards. As you climb the mountain, you may enter prairie meadows and patches of forest filled with piñon pine and juniper, where rock squirrels, mountain lions, and birds called piñon jays live. Still farther up are forests mainly of ponderosa pines, quaking aspens, and lodgepole pines, inhabited by golden-mantled squirrels, porcupines, and western bluebirds. Finally you'll reach an area where tall Douglas firs and Engelmann spruces tower over a quiet, needle-strewn forest floor. This forest is called the Canadian zone because it looks a lot like the taiga of Canada and Alaska. Bushy-tailed wood rats, three-toed woodpeckers, and Clark's nutcrackers make their homes here.

Near the mountaintop, where the air is colder and the wind is stronger, you'll notice that fir and spruce trees grow in stooped, twisted shapes. You are nearing the treeline, the boundary between the area where trees grow and where they don't. Above the treeline is the arctic-alpine zone, filled with low-lying grasses, wildflowers, lichen-covered rocks, and mouselike pikas. This area, also called alpine tundra, has much in common with the arctic tundra in Canada and Alaska. By climbing a mountain, you've reached biomes with features like those hundreds or even thousands of miles to the north.

WHERE DINOSAURS SWAM: THE GREAT PLAINS

Seventy to eighty million years ago, the Rocky Mountains did not exist. Elasmosaurus, a 32-foot- (10-meter-) long aquatic reptile, paddled through a tremendous inland sea that stretched from central Canada down through Nebraska, and into Texas. And *Quetzalcoatlus*, a flying reptile with a wingspan of more than 35 feet (11 meters), roamed the skies. Today, the sea is gone, but fossils of sea creatures and footprints of dinosaurs can be found in the former seafloor: the rocks of the Great Plains. These plains lie in the heart of the continent, between the Rocky and the Appalachian Mountains. They stretch from northern Canada to southern Texas. In the lower forty-eight United States, these plains are covered by prairie.

The prairie is not just grass. Here it blooms with an abundance of flowers.

The prairie states are grassy, windy, sometimes dusty, and generally flat. Here, wheat grows, cows graze, eagles soar, and prairie dogs dig underground networks of burrows, called towns. Blackbirds, meadowlarks, and sparrows sing and fly over the tall prairie grasses. Ducks nest along wetlands known as prairie potholes. Trees grow mostly along rivers—cottonwoods lining muddy banks. Prairies may be grassy, but they aren't like lawns. Mixed in with the grasses is a rainbow of beautiful flowers such as lilies, clovers, sunflowers, and coneflowers. On windy days, prairie grass ripples into waves, shining like the surface of the ocean. If you look carefully you may still see paths made by herds of bison that roamed these prairies two centuries ago.

PRAIRIE PARTICULARS

There are three main types of prairie: short-grass, mixed-grass, and tallgrass. The short-grass prairie begins just east of the Rocky Mountains. It's very dry because of the rain shadow formed by the Rocky Mountains. To the east, short-grass prairie gradually gives way to the moister, mixed-grass prairie, which has taller grasses, 2 to 4 feet (about 60 to 120 centimeters) tall. This land is suitable for growing relatively dry crops such as wheat. The easternmost prairie is the tallgrass prairie, which has grasses over 5 feet (1.5 meters) tall. Of the three types of prairies, the tallgrass region receives the most rainfall. When plowed, its soils are ideal for farming. Over many years, the deep roots of prairie grasses break up the dirt and decay, creating rich, fertile soil. This soil, plus ample rainfall, makes the tallgrass prairie one of the most productive farming areas in North America.

SAVE THAT SOIL

One challenge of living in the prairie is its periodic droughts, long periods without rain. In the 1930s, after several years of drought, Texas, New Mexico, Colorado, Kansas, and Oklahoma became known as the dust bowl. Without rain, the crops in the region died. As a result, their roots no longer held the soil in place. Strong winds blew the dried-out soil into the air, carrying millions of tons as far east as New York City! In the plains, blowing dust buried tractors, filled houses, covered people's clothes, and made breathing difficult. Since that time, some farmers have abandoned farming in the drier grassland regions of North America. Other farmers have changed when and how they plant and plow their fields, in order to keep the soil intact. Conserving soil by preventing it from blowing away or washing off during heavy rains is still a major concern today.

THE MIGHTY MISSISSIPPI-MISSOURI

One of the dominant features of the Great Plains region is the Mississippi-Missouri River system. The headwaters of the Missouri River are in southern Montana. From there the river flows through North and South Dakota; along the borders of Nebraska, Iowa, and Kansas; and then into Missouri, where it meets the Mississippi just north of St. Louis. The Mississippi River starts out in Lake Itasca, in northwest Minnesota, and flows all the way past New Orleans, Louisiana, where it meets the Gulf of Mexico.

When the rushing river meets the gulf, it slows down, losing energy. Suddenly, it cannot carry as much mud and sand. The river gradually drops sediment—the mud, sand and other material it picked up along its route—and deposits it on the seafloor. Over many years, these sediments have formed the wide, fanlike Mississippi Delta, at the tip of Louisiana.

Rivers such as the Missouri and Mississippi flood naturally from time to time, spreading water over low-lying, adjacent land, called floodplain. Every flood deposits sediment, making the soil good for farming after the water has receded. However, these floods also destroy bridges, wash away houses, submerge croplands, and kill people. Large floods may occur only every few decades—or even once in fifty or one hundred years. In between these floods, people crowd close to the river, establishing farms on the rich floodplain soil and building factories and homes along the riverside, despite the risks.

Over the years, people have tried to control flooding with dikes, levees, channels, and other structures that help direct the water flow away from towns and farms. But in tremendous floods, such as the Mississippi-Missouri flood of 1993, little can be done to stop the powerful water flow. Some landowners along the Mississippi-Missouri River system have tried to rebuild what they lost. Others have left the floodplain to build elsewhere. Part of the floodplain is also being left as a natural wetland, a place for the river to spread out during the next flood.

This used to be farmland, before the Missouri River broke through the levees and flooded the area.

A Look at Eastern North America

Beginning in late September, when the air is getting chilly and roadside stands are full of pumpkins, people stream out of cities in the eastern United States and flock to the countryside. They go to enjoy one of the earth's most spectacular sights: the colorful leaves of the temperate deciduous forest trees in fall. Looking out over the eastern mountains you can see the bright-red leaves of sugar maples, the burnt yellow of hickories, the deep purple of sweetgum trees, and the reds of oaks. This patchwork blaze of color is unique to eastern North America. Western North America, Europe, and Asia have some colorful trees in fall, but not as much of a variety of color or species.

The Colorful Forest

Temperate deciduous forest covers much of the Appalachians and the lowlands east of the Mississippi. Its trees are mostly deciduous—they drop their leaves during a short period in the fall. In contrast, narrow-leaved evergreen trees such as pines, spruces, and cedars drop their leaves only a few at a time, over the course of several years. Most temperate deciduous forest trees are broad-leaved, which means they have large leaves, as maples and oaks do. Although pine, spruce, and cedar trees are mainly thought of in connection with the taiga, some are found in the temperate deciduous forest.

Strangely enough, the oranges and yellows of fall leaves are actually hidden in the

31

*Thousands of tourists flock to New England every fall to see
the magnificent scenery as broadleaf trees turn brilliant colors.*

leaves all summer long. The chemicals that create these colors are masked by a green pig-
ment called chlorophyll, which plants use to capture energy from sunlight and make
food. In fall, when the leaves use up their last bits of chlorophyll, other colors such as
yellow and orange begin to show. Sugar in the leaf produces the red colors of maples and
oaks. Finally, the leaves fall and the trees remain bare until spring. Then, new leaves
emerge, and the cycle begins again.

SQUIRRELS AT WORK

Many trees you see in a temperate deciduous forest are planted by squirrels! They stash
acorns (oak nuts) and hickory nuts inside hollow trees and in the soil, so they can eat
them later. However, the squirrels do not dig up all the nuts they bury. So some sprout
and grow, becoming new trees.

THE APPALACHIAN ARK

In New Hampshire, they're called the White Mountains; in Vermont, the Green Mountains; in New York, the Catskills; in Pennsylvania, the Alleghenies; in Virginia, the Blue

EL NIÑO AND THE YEAR OF WILD WEATHER

Few North Americans will forget the wild weather of 1997–1998. In that year, North and Central America experienced an El Niño event, a change in global weather caused by a shift in ocean currents. In an El Niño year, which occurs every ten years or so, warm Pacific waters push close to South America, displacing a cool current that usually runs off the coast of Peru. In these years, the Peruvian fish industry collapses, as fishermen suddenly have trouble finding fish, which are usually plentiful in the cool current. Peruvians call this sea change El Niño, Spanish for "the child" because it arrives at about the same time as Christmas, the celebration of the birth of Jesus.

El Niño affects weather worldwide, causing droughts in Indonesia, floods in Chile, and heavy rains in Germany. In North America, the El Niño of 1997–1998 shifted weather patterns, bringing an extremely mild, warm winter to the upper and lower midwestern United States. Meanwhile, strong storms from the Pacific, full of moisture from warm El Niño currents, brought torrential rains to Mexico and Southern California. Floods washed roads away, houses slid off muddy, unstable hillsides, and beach houses were swallowed by high waves. These storms moved east all the way to Florida, causing flooding that ruined crops and damaged homes near Tampa. Central Florida's deadly tornadoes of February 1998 were also spawned by an El Niño–related storm.

The same storms that hit Florida that winter pushed up the Atlantic coast bringing snow to the Carolinas, and ice storms to New England. In the end, the winter of 1997–1998 was judged the strongest El Niño event on record. Meteorologists—scientists who study weather—are now trying to understand why El Niño events have occurred more often than usual in the 1980s and 1990s. Some scientists wonder whether this increased frequency of El Niño events is related to changes in global climate.

Ridge; in Tennessee, the Cumberland Mountains. All these names refer to parts of the Appalachian Mountains, which run from Newfoundland in Canada to Alabama in the southern United States. These mountains formed three to four hundred million years ago, when the tectonic plate carrying eastern North America collided with that of Europe and northwest Africa. The heat and pressure resulting from these collisions folded and raised the land. The Appalachians were once as high as the European Alps or maybe even the Himalayas. But since then, they have been worn down to gentle, low peaks. The highest peak in the Appalachian Mountains is North Carolina's Mount Mitchell, 6,684 feet (2,037 meters) high, less than half the height of the highest peak in the Rocky Mountains, Mount Elbert, at 14,433 feet (4,399 meters).

An Icy Refuge

During the last ice age, which ended fifteen thousand to ten thousand years ago, the southern Appalachians were a refuge for many animals and plants. The glacial ice did not reach the tops of the Appalachian Mountains. So on Appalachian mountaintops, and tucked into valleys, many species that died elsewhere survived. Scientists call these safe places glacial refugia. When the earth warmed again, the species spread out from there, populating other areas. The Appalachians today are still rich in species, with two thousand kinds of fungi, one hundred thirty kinds of trees, and fourteen hundred flowering herbs (plants with soft, nonwoody stems).

Weather Watchers

North America is an exciting place for watching weather. It experiences some of the most frequent and most dynamic storms on earth. For example, when cold air pushes southward from Canada and collides with warm, moist air moving northward from the Gulf of Mexico, strong storms arise. Thunderstorms, hail, and even tornadoes occur over the Great Plains.

Tornadoes are more common in the United States than anywhere else on earth, with as many as six hundred in a single year. On April 11, 1965, a system of thirty-seven tornadoes swept across Iowa, Wisconsin, Illinois, Indiana, Michigan, and Ohio, killing 271 people and injuring 3,000. The swirling winds of tornadoes can pick up and transport houses, railroad cars, and even people. (A woman, picked up by a tornado but set down unharmed, saw a cow fly by her in the air!) One early morning in February 1998, tornadoes touched down near Kissimmee, Florida, uprooting trees, ripping off roofs, tossing around vehicles and killing at least 35 people. The destruction, as is typical with tornadoes, was scattered. One row of houses, for instance, was destroyed, while the next row of houses was untouched.

Other North American weather events include hurricanes that develop in the Atlantic and then swirl across Florida and the Gulf Coast west to Texas. In the north, major snowstorms often strike the edges of the Great Lakes, and ice storms plague the northeastern United States. When cold air from Canada picks up moisture while crossing the Great Lakes, it can dump huge amounts of snow in such places as New York State. Meanwhile, in California, strong storms that develop in the Pacific bring heavy rains to California, causing floods and mudslides. During storms, pounding surf can wash away beaches and seaside homes, and cause cliffs to collapse. Keeping an eye on all these weather events makes North America's weather forecasters very busy. It's just one more element that makes the lower forty-eight United States a naturally dynamic place.

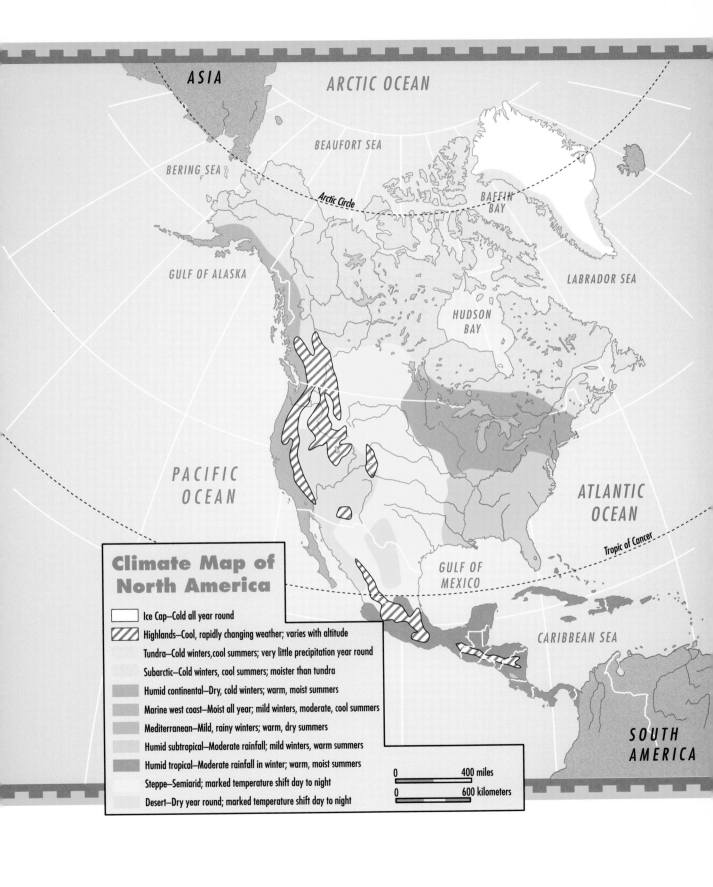

ASIA

ARCTIC OCEAN

BEAUFORT SEA

BERING SEA

Arctic Circle

BAFFIN BAY

GULF OF ALASKA

LABRADOR SEA

HUDSON BAY

PACIFIC OCEAN

ATLANTIC OCEAN

Tropic of Cancer

GULF OF MEXICO

CARIBBEAN SEA

Climate Map of North America

☐	Ice Cap—Cold all year round
▨	Highlands—Cool, rapidly changing weather; varies with altitude
	Tundra—Cold winters, cool summers; very little precipitation year round
	Subarctic—Cold winters, cool summers; moister than tundra
	Humid continental—Dry, cold winters; warm, moist summers
	Marine west coast—Moist all year; mild winters, moderate, cool summers
	Mediterranean—Mild, rainy winters; warm, dry summers
	Humid subtropical—Moderate rainfall; mild winters, warm summers
	Humid tropical—Moderate rainfall in winter; warm, moist summers
	Steppe—Semiarid; marked temperature shift day to night
	Desert—Dry year round; marked temperature shift day to night

SOUTH AMERICA

0   400 miles

0   600 kilometers

*When Popocatépetl, an active volcano near Mexico City,
erupts, it blankets the area—home to nearly thirty million people—
with ash and smoke.*

FOUR

MARVELOUS MEXICO

In Mexico you can walk through a desert of organ-pipe cacti or stroll along a sandy beach. You can climb a steep, snowcapped mountain or wander through a forest where monarch butterflies coat the trees. You can ride a horse through a grassland full of cattle or gaze across fields of orange marigolds that stretch for miles. You can boat down a river as howler monkeys howl and parrots chatter in the trees. Mexico has deserts, mountains, and beaches that may remind you of the southwestern United States. But it also has features such as tropical rain forests, cloud forests, and tropical deciduous forests that you'll find only this far south.

THE LAY OF THE LAND

Mexico covers 759,530 square miles (1,967,183 square kilometers), more than three times the area of California. It lies between the Pacific Ocean on the west and the Gulf of Mexico and the Caribbean Sea on the east. To the south, it borders the Central American countries of Guatemala and Belize. To the north, Mexico borders the United States. The Rio Grande, a river that Mexicans called Rio Bravo del Norte, forms the border between Mexico and Texas, before entering the United States and flowing through New Mexico.

CRADLED BY MOUNTAINS

Like the western United States and Central America, Mexico is mountainous and tectonically active—it experiences severe earthquakes and occasional volcanic eruptions. In

MEXICO CITY: SCENIC BUT SINKING

Almost seven hundred years ago, an ancient people called the Aztecs built a city called Tenochtitlán on an island in Lake Texcoco. Much later, in the 1600s, the lake was completely drained by the Spanish, who had conquered the region. Now called Mexico City, it has the second-largest population of the world's cities.

Home to one out of every four people in Mexico, the Mexico City area is crowded and growing. In 1995, it had an estimated population of 27.9 million, almost three times the size of Los Angeles. By the year 2000, Mexico City is expected to be the world's largest urban area. Although Mexico has many natural resources—minerals, oil reserves, wildlife, and rich soils—supporting such a tremendous city promises to be difficult.

Mexico City is located in the beautiful Valley of Mexico, which is ringed by snow-capped mountains. The city is 7,350 feet (2,240 meters) above sea level, so it has a cool, pleasant climate, with temperatures averaging 54°F (12°C) in January and only 63°F (17°C) in July. Unfortunately, the city's location has its disadvantages. It is adjacent to active volcanoes and prone to earthquakes. Rainfall is low, and water is scarce in the area. The city must pipe it in from far away, across the mountains that surround it. And many buildings, which sit on the soft lake bed, are slowly sinking.

In addition, air pollution from the city's cars, buses, and sixty thousand nearby factories sometimes gets trapped in the city's bowl-shaped valley, creating an unhealthy pollution buildup. This occurs during thermal inversions, when a layer of cold polluted air gets trapped underneath a layer of warm air. Because the layers don't mix much, pollution stays near ground level, forming a brown, choking smog. Steps are being taken to reduce pollution. For instance, each car owner is allowed to drive only on certain days of the week, reducing traffic and overall daily pollution. But there's much more to be done. This spectacular city, blessed with cultural attractions and a pleasant climate, nevertheless will face problems related to its growing population and its geographical location for many years to come.

1985, an earthquake killed ten thousand people in the capital, Mexico City, and did $4 billion in damage. In July 1997, a volcano named Popocatépetl, which means the "smoking warrior," erupted. Ash and smoke blanketed Mexico City, causing people to have difficulty breathing and forcing the airport to shut down temporarily.

In Mexico, the Sierra Madres, the southern extension of the Rockies, split into two mountain chains: the Sierra Madre Occidental, to the west, and the Sierra Madre Oriental, to the east. In between these ranges lies the Mexican Plateau, a raised area from 3,700 to 9,000 feet (about 1,125–2,750 meters) above sea level. About half of

The Sea of Cortez (Gulf of California), between the main part of Mexico and the Baja California peninsula, provides a study in contrasts: peaceful-looking blue-green water, windswept beaches with palm trees, and rugged hills.

Mexico is located in this high plateau. In central Mexico, the two mountain ranges meet the Sierra Madre del Sur, another mountain range. Together they form a large, raised "bowl" where Mexico City lies.

THIS IS NOT CALIFORNIA

Despite its name, Baja California is not part of the state of California. It's part of Mexico. It's one of the world's largest peninsulas, land areas surrounded on three sides by water. Baja California—Baja, for short—juts south from Tijuana into the Pacific Ocean for about 800 miles (1,290 kilometers). Many of Baja's beaches are lined with houses and high rises, but the region still has wild, undeveloped land. Most of Baja is very dry—sandy desert or a type of shrubby land called chapparal. Yet atop Baja's mountains are moist forests of pine and oak, and near the coast small swamps survive. Lizards, snakes, foxes, chipmunks, hummingbirds, and skunks are among the animals that inhabit the Baja Peninsula. There's even a kind of salamander that lives up in trees and squeaks like a mouse.

Between Baja California and the main part of Mexico is an inlet of the Pacific Ocean called the Gulf of California or the Sea of Cortez. In this beautiful gulf, you can snorkel with sea lions, sail among dolphins, and see fin, blue, gray, humpback, and sperm whales. Gray whales approach boats and even allow their faces to be rubbed by boat passengers! The calves of these whales are born here. Many animals and plants found on the islands and in waters of the Gulf of California are found nowhere else on earth.

EXPLORING THE NATURE OF MEXICO

Running along desert roads in Mexico and the southwestern United States are two animals of cartoon fame, coyotes and roadrunners. The 2-foot- (60-centimeter-) long birds hunt snakes, lizards, and other prey. Mexico also has much more wildlife in its nine major land biomes—desert, grassland-mesquite, oak-pine forest, thorn forest, cloud forest, boreal forest, chapparal, tropical deciduous forest, and tropical rain forest.

DRY BUT DELIGHTFUL

More than two-thirds of Mexico is arid or semiarid. That's because northern Mexico lies in the subtropics, where descending warm air masses dry the land, creating deserts. The Sonoran and Chihuahuan deserts, which lie mostly in Mexico, extend northward into Arizona and New Mexico. In these deserts, organ-pipe cacti and hundred-year-old saguaro cacti stand 50 feet (15 meters) tall, providing nesting places for woodpeckers, wrens, owls, and other creatures. At night, when the air is cool, kangaroo rats gather seeds, snakes hunt for mice, and bats drink nectar from cactus flowers.

In places that receive a little more rain, grasses dominate the land and mix with

*Money may not grow on trees, but epiphytes—air plants—do, in
the canopy of this Central American rain forest.*

mesquite, a fragrant tree in the bean family. Such grasslands are often cattle-grazing lands. The smoke from mesquite wood used on a grill gives meat a distinctive taste. Native people make flour, candy, cement, and dye from other parts of the plant.

FORESTS IN THE CLOUDS

The Mexican Plateau once had plentiful oak-pine forests. Many of them have been cut for timber and cleared for growing crops. In the remaining forests, huge, red-and-white woodpeckers still poke holes in trees, and raccoonlike coatis search for food.

Oaks also grow in cloud forests, mountaintop forests that are almost constantly bathed by clouds. Oddly, dogwoods, black gum, sweet gum, and American hornbeam trees, which are native to the forests of the eastern United States, grow in these cloud forests, as well. In this moist cloud forest biome, the trees become coated with mosses and bromeliads, relatives of the pineapple that grow perched on other plants. Some bromeliads' leaves form cuplike centers that fill with water, creating tiny pools where tadpoles live. Toucans, hummingbirds, deer, anteaters, foxes, and peccaries inhabit these forests.

Compared with some of the world's deserts, the Chihuahuan Desert of northern Mexico and southwestern United States looks like a garden.

Hordes of monarch butterflies gather at their winter home in the mountains of Michoacán, Mexico.

MOUNTAINS FOR MONARCHS

High up on other mountains are boreal forests with evergreen trees, much like the boreal forests in Canada and Alaska. In the boreal forests near Angangueo, northeast of Mexico City, monarch butterflies that migrate from Canada and the United States to a warmer climate gather to spend the winter. The Mexican government and local people are working to protect the "butterfly trees" by maintaining a Monarch Butterfly Ecological Preserve.

THE RAINY SOUTH

Although northern Mexico is rather dry, the southern part of the country is quite rainy. Rain forests grow on the low-lying limestone Yucatán Peninsula. Spider monkeys swing among the trees, and huge beasts called tapirs, with piglike snouts, search the ground for

MEXICO'S ANSWER TO THE GREAT DINOSAUR MYSTERY

Lying under the ground in Mexico's Yucatán Peninsula is the key to one of science's greatest mysteries. About sixty-six million years ago, dinosaurs, along with many other animal and plant species, became extinct—died out. For years, scientists wondered why.

In 1980, Luis Alvarez, a physicist from the University of California at Berkeley, discovered a large amount of a rare element named iridium in ocean sediments formed sixty-six million years ago. All over the world, rocks this age contained a lot of iridium, which is rather rare on earth. Alvarez knew that some meteorites, rocks that fall from space to earth, have lots of iridium.

He began to wonder if perhaps a very large meteorite, at least 6 miles (10 kilometers) in diameter, had hit the earth. The huge impact could have thrown dust, including iridium from the meteorite, up into the atmosphere. This dust would have spread around our planet. That may be why sediments formed then would contain relatively large amounts of iridium.

Is it a coincidence that this meteorite hit the earth at about the time the dinosaurs became extinct? Perhaps not. The layer of dust created by the meteorite would have blocked the sun, plunging the earth into darkness for several years. Plants, which need sunlight for photosynthesis, would have died. The animals that needed to eat the plants would have starved. Scientists also say the meteorite's impact would have had other side effects, including global cooling, tremendous amounts of acidic, corrosive rain, and widespread fires. (Sediments from that time contain much soot, created by fires.) All these changes in the earth's environment might have caused the dinosaurs to become extinct.

Scientists wondered, if there had been a meteorite, where did it fall? The crater had to be huge. A likely crater is at Chicxulub, in the Yucatán Peninsula of Mexico. Over the past sixty-six million years, the crater has filled in with sediment that, under pressure, formed rock. So it's not easy to see. But geologists have drilled down and found melted rock that shows where the meteorite hit. By current estimates, the buried crater is about 186 miles (300 kilometers) wide.

Scientists cannot prove that the climatic change triggered by the meteorite caused the dinosaurs to become extinct. But it seems likely that these two events, which occurred so close together in time, are closely linked.

---

fruit. These tropical rain forests extend southward into Central America, which will be discussed in Chapter 5. Another biome, tropical dry forest, occurs in both Mexico and Central America. Tropical dry forests have many of the plants and animals we associate with rain forests, but they experience a dry season, when many of the trees lose their leaves.

Land Without Summer

Unlike most of the United States, Mexico and Central America do not experience spring, summer, fall, and winter seasons. That is because these countries are closer to the equator, where sunlight shines almost directly on them year round, and the number of daylight hours changes very little. Mexico has two seasons, rainy and dry. In the rainy season, from June to October, thunderstorms usually occur every afternoon. During this time, plants grow quickly and flowers bloom. Deserts are suddenly carpeted in an incredible array of pink, blue, yellow, gold, and white wildflowers. Because of its location, Mexico is in the path of hurricanes that move inland from both the Gulf and the Pacific coasts during the rainy season. In the dry season, from November to May, some plant leaves turn brown and drop, while other plants die back.

During the dry season, *nortes*, cold air masses from the north, sometimes bring a few weeks of cold air and rain, causing a second rainy season. El Niño can also change weather patterns during Mexico's dry season, bringing lots of rain that causes desert flowers to bloom a second time that year.

View from the Borderlands

Many United States citizens' first and only impression of Mexico is from Nogales, Tijuana, Mexicali, or other Mexican border towns and cities. Americans travel to them on day trips by car for business or pleasure. Many Mexicans' first encounter with the United States is from day trips to border cities, too. Yet these border towns—bustling with trade, full of hopeful immigrants, and spiced by an exciting mix of cultures—have more in common with each other than with their home countries.

Beauty of the Borderlands

The borderlands, also called *la frontera*, encompasses an area roughly 60 miles (100 kilometers) on either side of the U.S.–Mexican border. The area holds some of the greatest natural treasures on the North American continent: deserts, valleys, and mountaintops with an incredible diversity of species of butterflies and birds. In southeast Arizona, forest-covered mountains poke up out of desert and dry grasslands. Scientists call these mountains sky islands because the animals and plants that live in the forests on these mountains are completely isolated from other wildlife by surrounding desert and grasslands. Bird-watchers from all over the world come to see hummingbirds and other colorful birds. Fortunately, parts of the borderlands are protected in reserves such as Organ Pipe Cactus National Monument in southern Arizona and Sierra del Pinacata in Mexico. Someday biologists may release Mexican gray wolves in this area, to join the mountain lions, bears, and other wildlife. Wolves once lived in this region but have died out.

DUMPING ON THE BORDER

All over the world there are problems with illegal immigration and trade across borders. People sneak across borders to find a better life, to smuggle goods that are cheaper in one country than in another, or to transport illegal drugs and other products. Residents of the U.S.–Mexican borderlands struggle not only with these issues but with a growing pollution problem.

Why are the borderlands so polluted? One reason is the many factories there. Many American companies have built factories on the Mexican side of the border. There are more than two thousand of these factories, called *maquiladoras*, mostly near Nogales. By operating in Mexico, companies can legally pay workers wages much lower than those in the United States. (Some workers make as little as $20 a week.) The companies can also release greater amounts of toxic pollution into streams, rivers, and the air, because Mexico's environmental laws are not as strong or as well enforced as in the United States. Finally, the companies can easily truck the goods they make across the border to the United States, where they can be sold at a good profit.

Because of these *maquiladoras*, high levels of toxins are showing up in the air, the water, and on the land. Pollution is also coming from the border towns themselves, many of which have little or no sewage treatment. To make matters worse, U.S. trucks from as far away as Colorado sneak into Mexico to dump their waste illegally. They do this to avoid paying to dispose of the waste properly in the United States.

These factors have resulted in pollution of the borderlands and the Rio Grande, which runs along the Texas–Mexico border. Fortunately, people have begun to work to clean up the region. In recent years, *maquiladoras* owned by large American companies have started to reduce their pollution and clean up their act. Smaller and midsized factories have been slower to make changes, but there's hope they will, too. To solve the problems of this region, people on both sides of the border will need to work together as North Americans.

At this plantation in Guatemala, coffee is still grown the old-fashioned way—in the shade.

FIVE

VITAL LINKS: CENTRAL AMERICA AND THE CARIBBEAN

Chances are, every day someone in your family sits down to a bit of Central America and the Caribbean. A morning cup of coffee, a banana on your cereal, a chocolate snack may all come from crops grown in these regions. Pumpkin pie, that Thanksgiving tradition, wouldn't be the same without nutmeg, a spice grown on the Caribbean island of Grenada. Even flowers in a vase might have been grown in Central America, then flown to your local florist. But Central America and the Caribbean have more than just fields for growing crops. These southern reaches of North America have breathtaking scenery, unique geology, and remarkable plant and animal communities.

CENTRAL AMERICA: HIGH AND LOW

Central America is a general term for a group of seven countries that lie in between Mexico and South America: Guatemala, Belize, Honduras, El Salvador, Nicaragua, Costa Rica, and Panama. Central America encompasses 202,265 square miles (523,865 square kilometers), about a quarter the area of Mexico. The region is home to thirty million people, not many more than the Mexico City area. Like Mexico, Central America is extremely mountainous, with several hundred volcanoes, many of which are active.

CLIMB UP TO GET COOL

Central America is in the tropics, close to the equator, so you might expect all of it would be warm. Some low-lying coastal areas along the Caribbean are hot and humid,

This mangrove forest, along the shore of Costa Rica, looks like a strange procession of skeletons.

with average temperatures of 80°F (27°C). But high up on Central American mountains, which can be 10,000 feet (more than 3,000 meters) tall, the weather is cold, and snow may cover the ground.

Most Central Americans don't choose either extreme, but instead live in the valleys between volcanoes, at altitudes of 3,300–6,500 feet (about 1,000–2,000 meters). With average temperatures of 60°–72°F (16°–22°C), the climate is cool and comfortable. Also, there aren't as many mosquitoes that carry diseases such as malaria and yellow fever as there are in more low-lying areas. Living in between volcanoes has its advantages. Ash from volcanoes fertilizes the soil, making crops grow well. Unfortunately, living at the foot of a volcano is also risky because of earthquakes and volcanic eruptions. Earthquakes hit Managua, Nicaragua, in 1972, Guatemala City in 1976, San Salvador in 1986, and southern Costa Rica in 1991, among others.

DIG THAT DIVERSITY

Costa Rica is about the size of West Virginia. Yet it has at least 830 bird species, more than Alaska, Canada, and the lower forty-eight United States combined. Two and a half acres (one hectare) of tropical rain forest in Central America may have two hundred species of trees, while a forest in Indiana may have only twenty or so. As these statistics demonstrate, species diversity, the number of different kinds of animals and plants, is generally much higher nearer the equator than nearer the North and South Poles. Scientists are not sure why there is such species diversity in the tropics. But the variety of orchids, ferns, beetles, frogs, birds, snakes, insects, and fish is not only fascinating for scientists to study but important to people throughout the world. Tropical rain forest plants and animals are sources of food, medicines, glues, dyes, and other products.

BELIEVE-IT-OR-NOT BIOMES

No matter where you stand in Central America, you're no more than 125 miles (200 kilometers) from the coast. Yet between you and that coast may be steep mountains, thick forests, rivers, lakes, grasslands, swamps, or other distinct areas. In Central America, different biomes exist close together, primarily because of the great variations in altitude. Soil, rainfall, and land use affect where biomes are located, too. How close together are tropical biomes? From San José, Costa Rica, you can drive three hours in one direction to reach a volcanic peak where you'll shiver even in a heavy sweater, or three hours in another direction to reach a lowland rain forest, where you'll sweat even in a T-shirt.

A BEAUTIFUL BIOME TOUR

To explore the biomes of Costa Rica, you could begin near the Pacific Ocean, where there are rocky shorelines, sandy beaches, mud flats, and mangrove swamps. Leaving the shore, you could reach the savanna, a grassland with widely scattered trees and grazing cows. Farther inland, on higher ground, you would find deciduous forest, with tall trees that drop their leaves during the dry season. If you were lucky, you might hear the rustling of an army ant swarm as it traveled through the dry forest leaves. Antbirds, birds that follow army ant swarms, prey on beetles, flies, and other creatures that fly up to escape the ants.

To examine more biomes, you could climb the Cordillera de Guanacaste, a mountain range with moist tropical forests. The upper mountain slopes are constantly bathed in clouds. In these cloud forests, colorful orchids grow, perched on mossy trees. Through the fog you might see a hovering hummingbird or a flash of deep-green feathers as a resplendent quetzal, a rare, sacred bird, flies from tree to tree. Atop some mountains you would find only barren fields of volcanic ash.

On the Caribbean side of the mountain, you would find some biomes that are different from those on the Pacific side. Below the cloud forest, you could walk through lowland rain forests and evergreen forests. Near the coast you would reach swamp forests and sandy beaches where sea turtles lay their eggs at the same time every year.

After all your hiking, you would have had only a small taste of Costa Rica's biomes. For instance, the highest mountains have additional biomes, such as oak forest and páramo, a treeless biome with mosses, low-growing plants, gnarled shrubs, and short bamboo.

ONE BIG SHARK SURPRISE!

Tropical North America has some spectacular natural features. For instance, in southwestern Nicaragua, Lake Nicaragua contains a biological surprise. This lake, the world's tenth largest, is home to the only freshwater sharks in the world! The lake also has other fish—swordfish, tarpon, and sawfish—that usually live in oceans, not in freshwater lakes. Scientists think that the ancestors of these fish swam in a bay of the Pacific Ocean. Lava from a huge volcanic eruption cut off the bay's connection to the ocean. This lava flow, plus a general uplifting of the land, created a salty lake. Over time, rivers flowed into the lake, making the water less and less salty. And over time, the fish species in the lake were able to adapt to the fresh water.

TROPICAL RAIN FOREST

Perhaps the most famous Central American biome is the tropical rain forest, which receives a lot of rain—at least 80 inches (200 centimeters) a year. The rain forest is home to tapirs, howler and spider monkeys, parrots, macaws, hummingbirds, poison-dart frogs, leafcutter and army ants, and other creatures. When you first walk through a tropical rain forest, you may wonder where all the animals are. You may not see any in the shady forest among the green trees, hanging vines, and tree ferns—which grow 20 feet (6 meters) or more tall.

Television shows and magazines often show close-up views of rain forest animals, but it takes time to see them in the wild. Many animals are perfectly camouflaged to match the color and shape of branches, trunks, and flowers in their surroundings. An

Layers of vegetation are evident in this Costa Rica tropical rain forest.

eyelash viper, a pencil-sized green snake, looks like a green twig when it's hanging on a branch. A slow-moving sloth, its fur covered with green algae, is well camouflaged up in a tree. Even blue morpho butterflies are hard to see when they're resting with their wings closed, showing only their dark outer sides. Yet when they slowly flap through the forest, their metallic blue inner wings are breathtakingly beautiful and easy to spot.

LAYER CAKE OF LIFE

Another reason rain forest animals can be challenging to find is that there are so many nooks and crannies where they can hide. Unlike a cornfield or rows of planted pine trees, a tropical rain forest has many layers of life. The base is the forest floor. Above the floor are understory plants, which grow well in the shade. On top is the rain forest canopy—the tops of trees, 40–70 feet (12–20 meters) high. This canopy forms the "roof" of the forest. Here and there, exceptionally tall trees such as cecropia stick up above the rest, forming an "emergent layer." Twining through the layers are hanging roots, vines, and lianas—woody vines—which act as aerial highways for snakes, iguanas, monkeys, and other climbers.

Despite all these layers of life, a tropical rain forest is fairly easy to walk through, because most of the plant growth is overhead, not on the shaded forest floor. Only where the sun pierces the canopy, where a tree has fallen, where a river runs, or where a road is cut, do plants grow into a thick, viny mass that's difficult to walk through.

Coffee, Birds, and Trees

If you drive through the highlands of Costa Rica, you'll see rows of coffee bushes stretching out over the hills. The beans they produce are roasted and used to brew the coffee people drink. Coffee beans are one of the most important cash crops in Central America. But the way people farm coffee has changed in recent years. And it's affecting everything from the coffee in North Americans' cups to the birds in North Americans' backyards.

Traditionally, coffee bushes were grown in the shade of tall trees. Families picked the coffee by hand and also harvested wood, fruit, herbs, and other products from the small plants and tall trees that grew around the bushes. Birds and other animals lived in the trees as well. As other forests were cut down for timber and to clear land for growing bananas and other crops, these coffee forests became a reservoir for birds. Many of these birds are neotropical migrants—birds that spend the summer in Alaska, Canada, or the lower forty-eight United States, then travel back to the tropics, including Mexico, Central America, the Caribbean islands, and South America. (Two-thirds of the bird species that spend the summer in the temperate deciduous forests of the eastern United States live the rest of the year in the tropics.)

In recent years, many farmers have started growing "sun coffee," because it is not so vulnerable to disease. It can be grown on bushes out in the sun. With the help of pesticides and fertilizers, it yields very large crops. Unfortunately, sun coffee does not provide families with the trees, fruits, medicinal herbs, and other products they get from the trees in the shade coffee plots. Sun coffee fields support very little wildlife, because they have no trees.

Many environmentalists, concerned about the decline of tropical birds, are trying to slow down or reverse the shift from shade coffee to sun coffee. They are working to help family farmers get their shade-grown coffee to market, and asking North Americans to buy it. Saving these plantations should help save birds that all North Americans share.

The Colorful Caribbean

With green mountains, white waterfalls, sandy beaches, and blue waters, some islands in the Caribbean Sea seem like a fantasy. The seven thousand islands found in the Caribbean form an archipelago called the West Indies. The islands form three main groups: the Bahamas, the Greater Antilles, and the Lesser Antilles. The Bahamas, made of coral, are actually located in the Atlantic Ocean east of Florida, not in the Caribbean Sea. But they are usually grouped with the Caribbean islands. The Greater Antilles are the tops of mountains that sank into the sea. Cuba, Puerto Rico, Jamaica, and

*The Grenadine Islands do their part in upholding the reputation
of the Caribbean Sea as a paradise.*

Hispaniola, an island that contains Haiti and the Dominican Republic, make up the
Greater Antilles. The Lesser Antilles contains much smaller islands that were formed by
underwater volcanoes spewing out lava and building up land that rose above the sea.
Some of these volcanoes are still active. In 1997, people fled their homes on the island of
Montserrat as the Soufrière Hills volcano erupted, burying two-thirds of the island in
ash and lava. The volcano, which began erupting in 1995, had been dormant for four
centuries.

COLORFUL CREATURES

Coral reefs surround many Caribbean islands. The reefs are large underwater ridges
made of limestone laid down by tiny soft-bodied creatures called corals. Corals live in
colonies that form a colorful, living layer on the surface of the reef, while building up

Some people think this Caribbean coral reef is even more breathtaking than nearby islands.

still more reef below. These coral reefs are home to an incredible diversity of creatures including parrotfish, angelfish, blowfish, octopuses, sharks, barracudas, lobsters, sting rays, and moray eels. In the coral reef biome, some animals depend on one another in very surprising ways. For instance, the cleaner fish gets its meals by nibbling the food particles stuck on the teeth of bigger fish!

Just off Belize is a tremendous barrier reef—a ridge of coral that parallels the mainland but is separated from it by a lagoon. This barrier reef, second in size only to the Great Barrier Reef of Australia, is a popular destination for SCUBA divers.

HOW PANAMA CHANGED THE WORLD

Between eighteen million and four million years ago, something happened to greatly affect the world: The narrow strip of land containing Costa Rica and Panama was born. Until then, what is now Mexico and the rest of Central America jutted down toward South America, but North and South America did not meet. Warm waters from the tropical part of the Atlantic Ocean and the Caribbean Sea flowed westward through the gap into the Pacific.

During the fiery birth of Costa Rica and Panama, underwater volcanoes spewed out lava, which cooled and hardened. The volcanoes grew higher, until finally they poked up out of the ocean, forming islands. Over time, lava from other eruptions spread out, joining the islands into the land we now know as Costa Rica and Panama.

The joining of North America and South America had widespread effects. Several kinds of animals, such as armadillos, porcupines, and possums, spread northward. Many more kinds of animals—squirrels, dog species, cat species, and deer—moved southward into South America. Llamas are the descendants of camels that spread south from North America to South America. Today 60 percent of the species found in South America are related to those animals from the north that went south!

The creation of Costa Rica and Panama not only joined two continents but separated two oceans. As a result, ocean animals on each side were cut off from one another. The ocean animals on each side evolved—underwent physical change—separately. Over time, they became so unlike one another that they are considered different species.

More dramatic were changes to the earth's climate. Warm tropical water that once flowed into the Pacific turned northward, creating the Gulf Stream. This warm water current flowed alongside what is now the United States; turned eastward, warming up Europe; then flowed south. In a complex climatic interaction, the current then dried out east Africa. What was once wet rain forest became dry desert and savanna.

And finally, the joining of North and South America had far-reaching effects on people. It enabled migration from north to south, and it put a whole new spin on the age of European exploration.

CONCLUSION

SEEING CONNECTIONS

North America, from Alaska to Panama, is linked in many ways. Some links are obvious, others hardly recognizable; but the links grow day by day.

A hundred years ago, boat travel from New York to San Francisco meant going all the way around Cape Horn, at the southern tip of South America. In 1914 the United States finished building the Panama Canal, which allowed travel between the Pacific and the Caribbean through the 51-mile (82-kilometer) canal. Land transportation improved considerably in the 1930s, with the Inter-American Highway, which runs from Texas to Panama City. Today, regular air flights take passengers and goods between Canada, the United States, Mexico, and Central American and Caribbean countries.

By boat, car, airplane, mail, telephone, fax, and E-mail, products and ideas now flow quickly throughout North America. Broccoli eaten in a Kansas kitchen today may have been grown and quick-frozen last week in Mexico before being shipped to the United States. Human intracontinental links are amazing, but the natural connections between regions of North America are even more intricate, ancient, and deep. Geologic faults, hurricanes, tornadoes, birds, and insects have always crossed national boundaries.

The bird a child sees in her backyard in Virginia may travel all the way to Guatemala, spend the winter there, then fly all the way back in spring, nesting in the same tree. A monarch butterfly flitting through fields in Indiana may be a descendant of butterflies that flew north from Mexico. Citizens of Canada, the United States, Mexico, and the Central American countries share many natural resources, from ocean fish to river water to migrating birds. The future of these natural treasures may depend on what kind of neighbors North Americans can be.

GLOSSARY

aurora borealis—Glowing bands of red, green, and white light occasionally visible in northern skies at night. The aurora borealis is caused by charged particles from the sun that interact with the earth's magnetic field.

biome—Area that has a specific kind of climate and a specific kind of community of animals and plants.

bromeliad—Member of the plant family Bromeliaceae; many bromeliads are epiphytes.

canopy—Second-highest rain forest layer, formed by the crowns of tall trees.

cloud forest—Rain forest that grows at middle to high elevations, on mountainsides, and is often bathed in clouds and mist; usually cooler, shorter, denser, and mossier than rain forests at lower elevations.

Cordillera—Mountains that run from Alaska through Panama to Tierra del Fuego, at the tip of South America. The Rockies and the Andes are a part of the Cordillera.

desert—Biome with less than 10 inches (25 centimeters) of precipitation each year.

epiphyte—Plant that grows on another plant but does not get its nutrients from that plant.

esker—Long, narrow ridge of sand, gravel, or boulders deposited by a stream within a melting glacier.

fjord—Narrow inlet of the sea between cliffs or steep slopes.

floodplain—Low-lying area covered by water when a river overflows its banks.

glacial refugia—Areas that were ice-free during an ice age and provided plants and animals with a place to survive this harsh climatic period.

glacier—Large mass of slow-moving ice.

global warming—Overall rise in the earth's air temperature. Scientists expect this rise in temperature will be felt unevenly, causing some areas to become warmer and others cooler. Global warming may be caused partly by industrial pollution that has led to a buildup of greenhouse gases around the earth.

Great Plains—North America's central region, which stretches between the Rockies and the Appalachians and runs from Canada to Texas.

greenhouse effect—Warming of the earth caused by gases that act like the glass panes of a greenhouse, allowing sunlight into the earth's atmosphere, but only allowing some of the sunlight-generated heat to escape.

greenhouse gases—Gases in the atmosphere that cause the greenhouse effect.

ice age—Period of global cooling, when glaciers build up and expand.

ice sheet—Glacier that spreads out over a large area.

permafrost—Permanently frozen ground.

polar desert—Cold, dry biome found at the North and South poles. A similar habitat is found on high mountaintops.

prairie—Term used for temperate grasslands in the United States and Canada.

prairie pothole—Relatively small freshwater wetland created by the action of glaciers on prairie lands.

rain shadow—Lack of rainfall on one side of a mountain. A rain shadow is created when moisture-laden air rises, cools, condenses, and rains down as it passes over a mountain, so that the air is dry by the time it reaches the other side.

sediment—Particles that are transported and deposited by wind, water, or ice.

taiga—Biome with conifers such as spruce, fir, and tamarack that occurs north of the temperate deciduous forest.

tectonic plate—Large piece of the earth's crust that slides over molten rock below, gradually shifting its position on the earth's surface.

temperate deciduous forest—Forest biome of the temperate zone with broadleaf trees that drop their leaves during the fall season.

temperate rain forest—Forest biome such as in the Pacific Northwest, that is cool and very rainy and where giant conifers grow.

thermal inversion—Condition that occurs when a layer of cooler air is trapped near the ground by a layer of warm air above. During thermal inversions, air circulation is decreased, and air pollution can be trapped close to the ground.

tropical deciduous forest—Forest biome near the equator that experiences a dry season in which its trees drop most of their leaves.

tropical rain forest—Forest biome of the tropics with warm temperatures, very heavy rainfall, and high species diversity.

tropics—Region close to the equator on either side, bounded by the Tropic of Cancer to the north and the Tropic of Capricorn to the south.

tundra—Biome found above the treeline. Tundra is characterized by soggy soil in summer, deep permafrost, and low-growing plants. Arctic tundra occurs in the Arctic; alpine tundra is found at high elevations.

Independent Countries in North America

Name	Capital
Antigua and Barbuda	St. John's
Bahamas	Nassau
Barbados	Bridgetown
Belize	Belmopan
Canada	Ottawa
Costa Rica	San José
Cuba	Havana
Dominica	Roseau
Dominican Republic	Santo Domingo
El Salvador	San Salvador
Grenada	Saint George's
Guatemala	Guatemala City
Haiti	Port-au-Prince
Honduras	Tegucigalpa
Jamaica	Kingston
Mexico	Mexico City
Nicaragua	Managua
Panama	Panamá
St. Kitts and Nevis	Basseterre
St. Lucia	Castries
St. Vincent and the Grenadines	Kingstown
Trinidad and Tobago	Port-of-Spain
United States	Washington, D.C

Dependencies in North America

Anguilla	Montserrat
Aruba	Netherlands Antilles
Bermuda	Puerto Rico
Cayman Islands	St. Pierre and Miquelon
Greenland (Kalaallit Nunaat)	Turks and Caicos Islands
Guadeloupe	Virgin Islands (U.S.)
Martinique	Virgin Islands (U.K.)

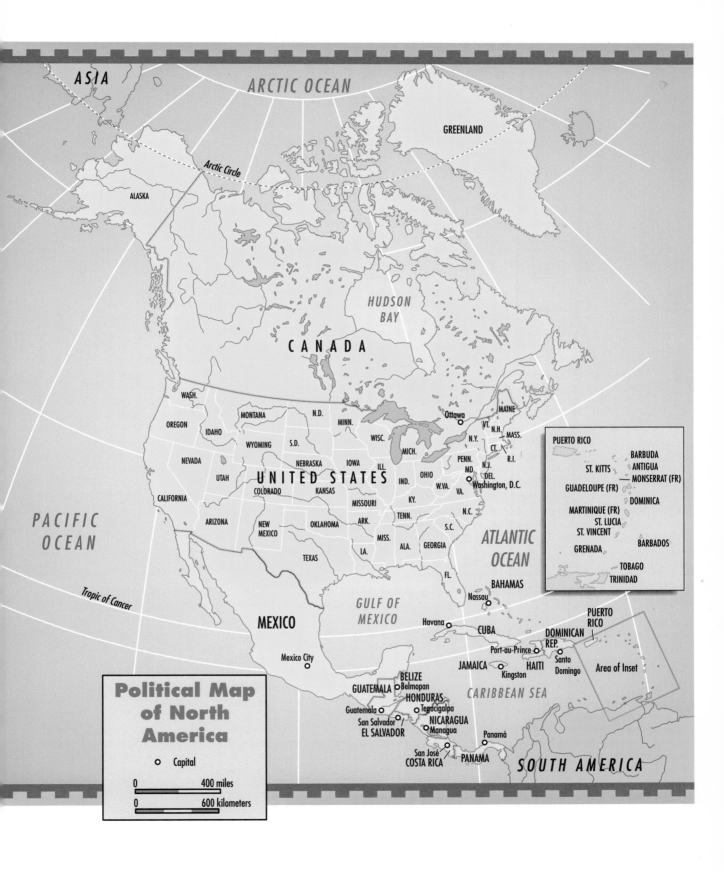

ASIA

ARCTIC OCEAN

GREENLAND

Arctic Circle

ALASKA

HUDSON
BAY

CANADA

WASH.

OREGON
IDAHO
MONTANA
N.D.
MINN.

Ottawa

MAINE

VT. N.H.
MASS.

WYOMING
S.D.
WISC.
N.Y.
CT. R.I.

NEVADA
NEBRASKA
IOWA
MICH.
PENN.
N.J.

UTAH
COLORADO
KANSAS
ILL.
IND.
OHIO
MD.
DEL.
Washington, D.C.

UNITED STATES
MISSOURI
KY.
W.VA.
VA.

PACIFIC
OCEAN

CALIFORNIA
ARIZONA
NEW
MEXICO
OKLAHOMA
ARK.
TENN.
N.C.

ATLANTIC
OCEAN

TEXAS
MISS.
ALA.
GEORGIA
S.C.

LA.

FL.

Tropic of Cancer

BAHAMAS

Nassau

MEXICO

GULF OF
MEXICO

Havana

CUBA

PUERTO
RICO

DOMINICAN
REP.

Mexico City

Port-au-Prince

Santo
Domingo

Area of Inset

JAMAICA
HAITI

BELIZE
Belmopan

Kingston

PUERTO RICO

BARBUDA
ANTIGUA

ST. KITTS

MONSERRAT (FR)

GUADELOUPE (FR)

DOMINICA

MARTINIQUE (FR)
ST. LUCIA
ST. VINCENT

GRENADA
BARBADOS

TOBAGO
TRINIDAD

GUATEMALA

HONDURAS

Guatemala
Tegucigalpa

San Salvador
EL SALVADOR
NICARAGUA
Managua

CARIBBEAN SEA

Panamá

San José
COSTA RICA
PANAMA

SOUTH AMERICA

**Political Map
of North
America**

○ Capital

0   400 miles

0   600 kilometers

FOR FURTHER READING

(Material for young readers is marked with an asterisk.)

BOOKS

* Agel, Jerome. *Where on Earth: A Refreshing View of Geography.* New York: Prentice Hall Press, 1991.

Benyus, Janine. *The Field Guide to Wildlife Habitats of the Eastern United States.* New York: Fireside, 1989.

————. *The Field Guide to Wildlife Habitats of the Western United States.* New York: Fireside, 1989.

Conrad, Jim. *Mexico: A Hiker's Guide to Mexico's Natural History.* Seattle: The Mountaineers, 1995.

Ferguson, Sue A. *Glaciers of North America.* Boulder, CO: Fulcrum 1992.

Forsyth, Adrian, and Ken Miyata. *Tropical Nature: Life and Death in the Rain Forests of Central and South America.* New York: Scribner, 1984.

Garrett, Wilbur E., ed. *Atlas of North America: A Space Age Portrait of a Continent.* Washington: National Geographic, 1987.

* Green, David R., ed. *The Eyewitness Atlas of the World.* London: Dorling Kindersley, 1994.

Kricher, John C. *A Field Guide to the Ecology of Western Forests.* Boston: Houghton Mifflin, 1993.

* Law, Kevin. *Places and People of the World: Canada.* New York: Chelsea House, 1990.

* Ouellet, Danielle, and others. *Discover Canada* (a series of books with titles on each province and territory). Toronto: Grolier Limited, 1993.

Perry, Donald. *Life Above the Jungle Floor.* New York: Simon & Schuster, 1986.

* Sayre, April Pulley. *Exploring Earth's Biomes* (a 12-book series on the biomes of North America): *Tropical Rain Forest, Desert, Grassland, Temperate Deciduous Forest, Taiga, Tundra, Ocean, Coral Reef, Seashore, Wetland, Lake and Pond,* and *River and Stream.*) New York: Twenty-First Century Books, 1995–1996.

Terborgh, John. *Diversity and the Tropical Rain Forest.* New York: W. H. Freeman and Company, 1992.

* van Rose, Susanna. *The Earth Atlas.* London: Dorling Kindersley, 1994.

* Wallace, David Rains. *The Monkey's Bridge: Mysteries of Evolution in Central America.* San Francisco: Sierra Club Books, 1997.

Wood, Robert W. *Science for Kids: 39 Easy Geography Activities.* Blue Ridge Summit, PA: TAB Books, 1992.

ARTICLES

Allen, William L. *Emerging Mexico: A Special Issue. National Geographic*, August 1996.

Bass, Rick. "The Heart of a Forest." *Audubon*, January–February 1992, 39–49.

Canby, Thomas Y. "Earthquake: Prelude to the Big One?" *National Geographic*, May 1990, 76–105.

Dibble, Sandra. "The Song of Oaxaca" (Mexico). *National Geographic*, November 1994, 38–63

Dollar, Tom. "Along the Mexican Border." *Arizona Highways*, October 1993, 14–38.

MAPS INSERTS IN *NATIONAL GEOGRAPHIC* MAGAZINE

Alaska, May 1994.

Ancient Mesoamerica, December 1997.

Central America, April 1986.

Earth's Dynamic Crust and *The Shaping of a Continent: America's Active West*, August 1985.

The Earth's Fractured Surface and *Living on the Edge*, April 1995.

The Making of Canada: Atlantic Canada, October 1993.

The Making of Canada: Ontario, June 1996.

The Making of Canada: Quebec, March 1991.

North America in the Age of the Dinosaurs and *Dawn on the Delta: 74 Million Years Ago*, January 1993.

INDEX

Page numbers in *boldface italics* refer to illustrations.